MW00641951

# The Christmas Frolick; or, Mirth for the Holidays

*2*

# THE
# CHRISTMAS FROLICK;
## OR,
## MIRTH for the HOLIDAYS.

### CONSISTING OF

A great Number of *admirable Stories* never before
printed ; with a felect Collection of others,
from *rare, old,* and *fcarce* Books.

With a Variety of NEW SONGS, written on pur-
pofe for this Work, and adapted to *well known
Tunes*

Likewife a felect Store of *New Jefts, Anecdotes,
Whims, Oddities* &c copied as fpoken by our
*Firft-rate* Wits , and never yet offered to public
Infpection.

The whole calculated to warm the Imagination,
raife the fpirits in the gloom of Winter, and
procure, what every one wifhes,

A MERRY CHRISTMAS, and a HAPPY NEW YEAR

---

*Who'd fail to be merry that cou d be ?
Who d wifh to be dull in dull Weather ?
Let us all be as gay as we fhou'd be
And fing and tell Stories together.*

---

## LONDON:

Printed for G ALLEN, in *Paternofter Row,* and
fold by all Bookfellers, Stationers, and News-
Carriers. 1775.

( Price One Shilling. )

( iii )

# TO THE

# R E A D E R.

IF the following Collection should be
found to anfwer, in any degree, the
Title of our Book, it is prefumed that no
Apology need be made for its Publication,
at this Seafon of Mirth and Feftivity.
Story-telling is a great help and Life to
Converfation. We have endeavoured to
felect fuch Stories from the beft Writers,
as will not difgrace thofe who relate them.
Indeed feveral of them are totally new,
and it muft be left to our Readers whether or not they think proper to make
thofe the fubject of their Narrations.
Almoft all our Songs and Jefts are alfo
fuch as have never been printed before.
The Anecdotes and Characters are written by the ableft Hands this Kingdom
ever produced; it need fcarcely be faid
that

that ADDISON is the Author of many of them,

Nothing now remains but to wish our Readers as many MERRY CHRISTMAS-TIDES, and as many HAPPY NEW YEARS as Health, Plenty, and good-humour, can jointly promise, or procure.

STORY

# STORY I.

## A Christmas Tale.

IN the Year 1753, a large and respectable Company of young Ladies and Gentlemen were affembled to fpend the Chriftmas Day, at the Houfe of Colonel Woodford, in Hampfhire. The Colonel had been a gay Man in his time; but his Ideas were elegant, his Sentiments pure, and his Heart uncontaminated by his commerce with the World.—His Eftate was ample, and the œconomy with which he manag'd it did him fingular honour. His fiift Pleafure was to fee his own Family happy, his fecond to make happy thofe around him.—When the Family had dined, the chearful Glafs had circulated, Tea and Coffee had been drank, and even Cards grew tirefome, the Company viewed Colonel Woodford with anxious Eyes, as hoping from his good Senfe and Expe-

A                                    rience

rience, a more rational Entertainment
than Feasting or Card-Playing could af-
ford. The Colonel read their Wishes in
their Looks, and without waiting for far-
ther entreaty, said, " Let us chat an Hour,
" my Boys and Girls. What think you of
" Story-telling for a Christmas Amuse-
" ment? I will tell you a Piece of the
" History of my own Life, (thank God
" and my Harriet it has been a happy
" Life thus far,) and you shall take a Les-
" son from our Conduct for your own, if
" you think our Example worthy of being
" copied."—The Company expressed their
Wishes that he would proceed ; which he
did to the following Purport.

" I was the younger Son of the Revd.
Dr. Woodford, of Staffordshire To say
any thing of my Father would be saying
too little, unless I bestowed on him all the
Praises due to Humanity elevated to the
highest degree of Perfection.—I was intended for the Church ; and of consequence educated so as to prepare my pas-
sage to the University ; but my Inclination
leading me to the Profession of Arms, I
prevailed on my Grandfather to purchase
me a Cornetcy in a Regiment of Horse.
It

It would be as impertinent to this Company, as troublesome to myself, to relate
by what gradations I rose almost to the
first Honours of my Profession. Suffice it
to say that I was not deficient in what I
thought the discharge of my Duty, and
that my gracious Sovereign has more than
rewarded my Endeavours. In the Year
1733, I was quartered in the City which
gave Birth to my Harriet. I had then never seen her: but an Accident, which for
that reason I shall ever deem propitious,
introduced me to her knowledge. A Company of Players had taken up their Resi-
dence, to entertain us during the Christmas Holidays —Accident placed me in
the same Box with my Harriet.—The
House was crowded; for the People of
Fashion had made a Point of attending,
to enable the Actors to feast thro' the Season of Festivity. In the Middle of the
fourth Act, the Word *Fire* occurred in
one of the Lines. The Actor spoke with
too elevated a tone of Voice A Lady who
heard, but did not understand him, mis-
took the elevation of his Voice for a cry
of " Fire."—The alarm soon spread, and
ill-founded as it was, spread with Rapi-

dity.

dity.—Every one was anxious to fave him
or herfelf.—A Coxcomb Lover (pardon
me, my dear) who attended mv Harriet,
ran off in the firft hurry, and left his precious Charge behind him.—My Eyes had
before drank in the bewitching Charms of
her Beauty—She was hurrying to the Door:
I faw the danger of her being crufhed to
death ; and preffing to her Affiftance, re-
pell'd, by mere force, the weight of feveral People that would have fallen on her.
—I catched her in my Arms, and crying,
" Tis all a miftake, Madam"—repeated
the whole Sentence of the Play in which
the Word *fire* occurred.—By this time two
of the Players had come forward, and af-
fured us that we were fafe.—With diffi-
culty I prevented my Harriet from faint-
ing.—She recollected herfelf, and remain-
ed in her Place.—Of thofe who crowded
to get out, feveral were terribly bruifed,
two had their Limbs broke, and one was
killed. A Lady who received no apparent damage at the time, languifhed for
two Months and then died.—I had the honour of attending my Harriet to her Father's, and received too many acknow-
ledgments for having conferred a common
Obligation.

Obligation. I was honoured with an Invitation to visit the Family—the cowardly Lover never renewed his Visit; not even to enquire after the Lady's Health. Suffice it to say, that I was honoured with her Confidence——Her Love—within three Months I was made the happiest Man living; and if my Charlotte bowing to his Daughter) continues, as she has begun, to copy her Mother's excellent Example, she cannot fail of becoming one of the happiest of Women."

This Tale, which was intended merely as a Christmas Entertainment, was productive of a very agreeable Consequence. Among the Company present was Sir George Newport. His Eyes struck fire at the Praises the Colonel bestowed on Charlotte.—He loved her on the Instant. — There could be no Objection to Sir George's Birth, Fortune, Person, or Character.—A speedy Marriage ensued; and last June made Colonel Woodford one of the happiest Grandfathers in the World.

A 3 STORY

## STORY II.

Account of an Uncle wrongfully Executed.

A Gentleman died poſſeſſed of a very conſiderable Fortune, which he left to his only Child, a Daughter, and appointed his Brother to be her Guardian, and Executor of his Will The young Lady was then about Eighteen; and if ſhe happened to die unmarried, or, if married, without Children, her Fortune was left to her Guardian and to his Heirs. As the Intereſt of the Uncle was now incompatible with the Life of the Neice, ſeveral other Relations hinted, that it would not be proper for them to live together. Whether they were willing to prevent any occaſion of ſlander againſt the Uncle, in caſe of the young Lady's death; whether they had any Apprehenſion of her being in danger; or whether they were only diſcontented with the Father's diſpoſition of his Fortune, and therefore propagated Rumours to the prejudice of thoſe who poſſeſſed it, cannot be known;
the

the Uncle, however, took his Neice to his House near Epping Foreſt, and ſoon afterwards ſhe diſappeared.

Great enquiry was made after her, and it appearing, that the Day ſhe was miſſing, ſhe went out with her Uncle into the Foreſt, and that he returned without her, he was taken into Cuſtody. A few days afterwards he went through a long Examination, in which he acknowledged that he went out with her, and pretended that ſhe found means to loiter behind him as they were returning Home ; that he ſought her in the Foreſt as ſoon as he miſſed her ; and that he knew not where ſhe was, or what was become of her. This Account was thought improbable, and his apparent Intereſt in the death of his Ward, and perhaps the petulant zeal of other relations, concurred to raiſe and ſtrengthen Suſpicions againſt him, and he was detained in cuſtody.

Some new Circumſtances were every day riſing againſt him. It was found that the young Lady had been addreſſed by a neighbouring Gentleman, who had,
a few

a few days before she was missing, set out on a Journey to the North; and that she had declared she would marry him when he returned: that her Uncle had frequently expressed his disapprobation of the Match in very strong terms: that she had often wept and reproached him with unkindness, and an abuse of his Power.

A Woman was also produced, who swore that on the Day the young Lady was missing, about Eleven o'Clock in the Forenoon, she was coming through the Forest, and heard a Woman's Voice expostulating with great eagerness; upon which she drew nearer the Place, and, before she saw any Person, heard the same voice say, *Don't kill me, Uncle, don't kill me;* upon which she was greatly terrified, and immediately hearing the report of Fire-Arms very near, she made all the haste she could from the Spot, but could not rest in her Mind, till she had told what had happened.

Such was the general impatience to punish a Man, who had murdered his Neice to inherit her Fortune, that upon
this

this evidence he was condemned and executed.

About ten days after the Execution, the young Lady came Home. It appeared, however, that what all the Witnesses had sworn was true, and the Fact was found to be thus circumstanced :—The young Lady declared, that having previously agreed to go off with the Gentleman that courted her, he had given out, that he was going a journey to the North ; but that he waited concealed at a little House near the skirts of the Forest, till the Time appointed, which was the Day she disappear'd. That he had Horses ready for himself and her, and was attended by two Servants also on Horseback. That as she was walking with her Uncle he reproach'd her with persisting in her Resolution to marry a Man of whom he disapproved, and after much Altercation, she said with some heat, *I have set my heart upon it, if I do not marry him it will be my death ; and don't kill me, Uncle, don't kill me :* that just as she had pronounced these Words, she heard a fire-arm discharged very near her, at which she started, and immediately afterwards

afterwards faw a Man come forward from among the Trees, with a Wood-Pigeon in his Hand, that he had juft fhot. That coming near the Place appointed for their rendezvous, fhe formed a pretence to let her Uncle go on before her, and her Lover being waiting for her with a Horfe, fhe mounted, and immediately rode off. That inftead of going into the North, they retired to a Houfe, in which he had taken Lodgings, near Windfor, where they were married the fame Day, and, in about a Week, went a Journey of Pleafure to France, from whence when they returned, they firft heard of the Misfortune which they had inadvertently brought upon their Uncle.

The Reader will need no other arguments than what are comprized in the above Narrative, (which is unqueftionably true) to convince him of the extreme Caution that ought to be made ufe of, before any Perfon is convicted on circumftantial Evidence, however ftrong, and apparently fatisfactory.

STORY

## STORY III.

A Stag Lives, after being shot through the Heart.

IN 1686, as Frederick William, Elector of Brandenburgh, and his Electress were hunting, they saw a Stag, at which the Electress took aim, and shot him with a leaden Bullet. He walked off 400 Yards, and crawled into a Ditch. The Elector's Gun-Smith followed him, and lodged a Ball in the back Part of his Head: Still, however, he kept his Legs, 'till a third was lodged under his left Ear, when he fell as dead. A Cart was sent for, which was three quarters of an Hour before it was brought. The Country Fellows turned him from one Side upon his Belly, and laying hold of his Horns, lifted his Head into the Cart, when, just as they were on the point of raising the Body, the Stag got on his feet, sprung away from them, and traversed the Fields with incredible Swiftness. He was pursued by Hounds, who more than once surrounded him, and the

Forrester

Forrester coming up, fhot him in the hinder Part of the Back; ftill, however, he attempted another efcape; but was feized and killed by the Dogs. On ex-amination it appeared that the Bullet which the Electrefs firft difcharged, went through the Heart of the Animal.

*⁕*⁕*⁕*⁕*⁕*⁕*⁕*⁕*⁕*⁕*⁕*⁕*⁕*⁕*

## STORY IV.

Cuftom of making Freemen of *Alnwick* Common, *Northumberland.*

THE Perfons that are to be made free, or, as they call it, *to leap the Well,* affemble in the Market-Place very early in the Morning, on the 25th of April. They are on horfeback, with every Man a Sword by his Side, dreffed in White, with white Night Caps, and attended by the Four Chamberlains, and the Caftle Bailiff, who are alfo mounted and armed in the fame Manner. From the Market-place they proceed in great order, with Mufic playing before them, to a large dirty Pool, called the *Freemens Well,*

*Well*, on the Confines of the Common. Here they draw up in a Body at some distance from the Water, and then all at once rush into it, and scramble through the Mud as fast as they can. As the Water is generally breast high, and very foul, they come out in a most filthy Condition; but dry Cloaths being ready for them on the other Side, they put them on with all possible Expedition, and then taking a Dram, remount their Horses, and ride full gallop round the whole Confines of the District; of which, by this Atchievement, they are become free.

After having compleated this Circuit, they again enter the Town Sword in hand, and are met by Women dressed up with Ribbons, Bells, and Garlands of Gum-Flowers. The Heroes then proceed in a Body till they come to the House of one of their Company, where they leave him, having first drank a Dram ; the remaining Number proceed to the House of the second, with the same Ceremony, and so on, till the last is left to go Home by himself.

B                              The

The Houfes of the new Freemen aie on this Day diftinguifhed by a great Holly Bufh, which is planted in the Street before them, as a Signal for their Friends to affemble, and make merry with them at their return —This ftrange Ceremony is faid to have been inftituted by King John, in Memory of his having once bogged his Horfe in this Pool, now called the *Freemens Well.*

## STORY V.

### Remarkable Inftances of Longevity.

HEnry Jenkins, an Englifhman, died in the year 1670. aged 169.—John Rovin, born at Szatlova Caranfbetcher, in the banat of Temefwai, lived to the age of 172, and his wife to 164, having been marned together 147 Years, and their youngeft fon being 90 at his Father's death. ——Peter Zorten, a Peafant of Keverefch, alfo in the banat of Temefwar, died on the 5th of January 1724, aged 185, the youngeft

youngeſt of his Children being then 97.
This Zorten fed only on pulſe.

## STORY VI.

### The Hiſtory of Will Wimble.

WILL Wimble was the Son of Sir
Richard Wimble, of Worceſter-
ſhire, who dying, Will's eldeſt brother
ſucceeded to the Eſtate for no other reaſon
but that he was the eldeſt; and Will was
left to ſeek his Foitune in any way that
would not diſgrace his Family.—He had
no inclination to the Pulpit, for he did not
love reading; Phyſic was his averſion;
while he had too much conſcience for the
Law, and too much compaſſion for the
Army. A mercantile Trade ſuited his
Genius, and was the object of his Wiſhes;
but that his Father denied him, and was
angry that he ſhould think of introducing
buying and ſelling into his Family The
Plan that Will laid down for his ſuppoit,
and at the ſame time to render himſelf a-
gieeable, is a proof of his good ſenſe and
address.

addrefs.—He was a perfect Mafter of all
thofe little Arts in which our Countrv
Gentry delight. He hunted a pack of
Dogs better than any Man in the Country,
and was very famous for finding a Hare:
He made a May-fly to a Miracle, and
furnifhed the whole Neighbourhood with
Fifhing-rods and Tobacco-ftoppers He
carried a Tulip-root from one to another,
and exchanged a Puppy between two
Friends, who lived at a Diftance, with
great Dexterity. The young Heirs he
frequently obliged with a net of his own
Weaving, a fetting-dog that he had himfelf inftructed, a Quail-pipe, or a new
Lafh for a Whip. The Mothers and Sif-
ters he generally complimented with bat-
tledores and Shuttlecocks or a Pair of
Garters of his own Knitting, and, whenever he met them, excited much Mirth by
enquiring " how they wore," and by
" afking Permiffion to tie them up." He
compofed all Differences between Gentlemen and their Servants; and tho' he
never gave the Footmen a Shilling, they
ftood more in awe of him than of their
own Mafters.—Such was the harmlefs
Life of Will Wimble, who lived better
                                    without

without any Fortune, than his booby
Brother did on four thoufand a Year.

✳✳✳✳✳✳✳✳✳✳✳✳✳✳✳✳✳✳✳✳

## STORY VII.

### An Inftance of the Ridiculous.

" AMong the many People who have
" had Courage and Learning to lay
" Ghofts, *G. W. Salomine*, may be reckon-
" ed and efteemed the moft confiderable
" and knowing ; for he made a Fortune
" and raifed an Eftate by this very Trade ;
" and is faid to have laid 1379 Souls in
" Red Sea . A Place which I know by
" Experience, and by Exam nation have
" found all Ghofts and Spirits are moft a-
" fraid of ; and this I think proves Salo-
" mine's Power to be very great, as it is
" a Place they would not but by force
" have went into.

" It is to be remarked that Salomine
" was the feventh Son of his Father and
" Mother, who was a virtuous Woman ;
" and he had alfo a wonderful faculty of
" curing all Difeafes *with a touch.* Such
B 3 " furprifing

" furprifing Power is there in fome Peo-
" ple. Yet this Gentleman was not more
" to be thought of than an Acquaintance
" of mine, an Oxford Scholar, who to
" my certain knowledge and belief had
" cured many Diforders and allayed the
" Ghofts of many difturbed People, when
" no other Perfon could do them.

   " In a Village where I lived, I do know
" there was a great Houfe, a Manfion-
" houfe, haunted by a fpirit that turned
" itfelf into a thoufand Shapes and Forms;
" but generally came in the figure of a
" *boiled Scragg of Mutton,* and had baffled
" and defied the learned Men of both Uni-
" verfities; but this being told to my
" Friend, who was a defcendant and rela-
" tion of the learned Friar Bacon, he un-
" dertook to lay it, and that even without
" his Books; and 'twas done in this Man-
" ner: He ordered fome Water to be put
" into a clean Skellet that was new, and
" had never been on the Fire. When the
" Water boiled, he himfelf pulled off his
" Hat, and Shoes and then took feven
" Turnips, which he pared with a fmall
" Penknife, that had been rubbed and
                " whetted

" whetted on a Loadstone, and put them
" into the Water. When they were boil-
" ed, he ordered some Butter to be melt-
" ed in a new glazed earthen Pipkin, and
" then mashed the Turnips in it. Just as
" this was finished, I myself saw the
" Ghost, in the form of a *boiled Scragg of*
" *Mutton*, peep in at the Window, which
" I gave him notice of, and he stuck his
" Fork into him, and sowsed both him
" and the Turnips into a Pewter Dish,
" and, eat both up; and the House was
" ever afterward quiet and still. Now this
" I should not have believed, or thought
" true, but I stood by and saw all the
" whole Ceremony performed."

The above monstrous Absurdity, which
will serve very well for a Holiday
Laugh, is copied from JACKSON's
*State of the Defunct.* Page 97.

STORY

## STORY VIII.

### The Lottery, a Christmas Tale.

A Young Lady in Lincolnshire, whom
we shall call *Lucinda*, was addressed by several young Fellows, who
pretended a great regard for her Person,
independant of all pecuniary Considera-
tions, because she was supposed to be rich.
During the warmth of their Addresses her
Father died Insolvent and she instantly
lost all her Admirers but Mr. Freeland,
who then, more earnestly than ever, pres-
sed her to honour him with her Hand in
Marriage; but the generous *Lucinda* dis-
dained to impoverish the only Man who
had given any solid proof of his Affection
for her    Just at this juncture an Uncle
of Lucinda's died in a distant Country,
and left her 12,000l.—It was unknown
to her Lovers that she had any such Relation, and she was determined to keep it a
secret for the present; but as the Lottery
was then drawing she caused it to be propagated

pagated (by Friends whom she could trust)
that she had got one of the 10,000l.
Prizes. Her Lovers instantly renewed
their Addresses, and were warmer in their
Adulation than ever. Freeland was the
only one who did not now implore the
Honour of her Hand, as he scorned to have
it thought that he courted her from interef-
ted Motives. In a few days it wa anoun-
ced in the News-papers who was the real
Poffeffor of the 10,000l. Prize: on which
Lucinda's Lovers again left her, and
calumniated her in every Company, as a
Jilt that would have entrapped them into
Matrimony. Lucinda now sent for Freeland, explained the real State of her Af-
fairs, and soon afterwards made him happy in the Poffeffion of herself, and the
12,000l which her Uncle had left her.
What heightens the Beauty of this Story
is, that Mr Freeland obtained a Prize
of 5000l. in that very Lottery, which,
as his Fortune was ample, he settled on
Lucinda the Day preceeding their Marriage.


STORY

## STORY IX.

### The ALMANACK ; or the Fortune-Teller, a New Year's Tale.

THREE young Ladies, with the ſame Number of young Gentlemen, who paid their Addreſſes to them, were on a Viſit at a Merchant's in the City, on the firſt of January, 1774, when after the circulation of a chearful Glaſs, the Merchant who was a Gentleman of ſingular Vivacity, told the young Ladies that his Father was a Fortune-Teller, and that he had in his youth, acquired Part of the old Gentleman's Art, " and now " (ſaid he) my Girls, if you will each of " you tell me the Day of your Birth, I " will tell you a Piece of good Fortune ; " if you, in return, will promiſe to do " all in your Power to verify my pre- " dictions." The Challenge was laughably accepted ; but he made them promiſe him ſeriouſly, and having learnt their reſpective Birth-days, told that they ſhould

should be severally married on the next return of that Day in the Almanack. The
Lovers took Advantage of the young
Ladies Promises: the Merchant insisted
on their " doing all in their Power to
" verify his Predictions;" and the Consequence was that within Six Months
Three Couple were made happy.

## STORY X.

### The HAUNTED HOUSE; a Twelfth-
day Tale.

ON Twelfth Night, in the Year,
1771. a large Company was assem-
bled at the Seat of Edmund Williams,
Esq. in Berkshire, to partake of the usual
Diversions of the Evening. When Sup-
per was over, and the Twelfth-Cake had
been shared, with the customary Scene
of Frolic, The Company began to think
of departing; but as the Weather proved
unfavourable, and most of the Company
had a considerable way home, Mr. Williams accommodated as many of them as
                                    possible

possible with Beds; but there was still one young Gentleman (Captain Darnley) unprovided for, and Mr. Williams frankly told him he had no room in which to lodge him, but one that was supposed to be haunted, and though (continued he) I have no Idea of such nonsense myself, we never yet could get any person to lodge in that Room. Young Darnley said he should be proud of lodging in such a Room; and Preparations were immediately made for his Reception, a good Fire being Lighted, and a Candle placed on a Table near it. The Captain retired to rest, and after reflecting an Hour on the oddity of his situation, fell asleep. About three o'Clock he was awakened by the opening of the Chamber Door, and not a little surprized to see a genteel Figure in White Walk slowly towards the Bed. The Candle burnt dim, and the Captain, with all his Courage, was too much alarmed to judge what the Apparition was. At length it turned down the Bed Cloaths, and came softly into Bed. The Captain found that it breathed, and was then less Terrified. At length he extended his Arm towards it, and felt a Finger, from which

which he flipped a Ring. Soon afterwards the Ghoft left the Bed, ftalked
flowly acrofs the Room, and fhut the
Door after it. The Captain flept in tran-
quillity during the remainder of the Night,
and in the Morning, when the Company
were affembled at Breakfaft, he afked if
any Perfon prefent had loft a Ring. Mifs
Williams declared herfelf Miftrefs of it ;
on which Dainley related the Particulars
of the Vifit of the Ghoft, not a little
to the confufion of the young Lady.—
Mr Williams took up the Matter in a frefh
Point of View, and faid that as his
Daughter had gone to Bed to the Captain without her Knowledge, it fhould
be his Fault if he did not go to Bed to
her in return. The Captain moft joyfully
accepted the Terms ; a happy Marriage
foon enfued, and he has called his Lady
by the Name of his *Dear Ghoft* ever
fince.


C          STORY

# STORY XI.

## The BLUNDERER.

AMong that Species of Blunderers who say a good Thing without knowing it, may be ranked Mr *Bush*, who being one Day in the Fields with his Companions, they were suddenly catched in a violent Shower of Rain, and ran with all Speed to the Hedge for Shelter. A young Lady passing by at the Instant, our Hero cries out to her, " Whither so " fast in all this Rain, my dear ? You " had better come here, and take shelter " under a *Bush*." — " Well said, Jack, " cries his Companions.— that's the smart- " est Thing that ever came out of thy " Mouth."—Jack was mightily elated with the Applause that was paid him, though he knew not where the Cream of the Jest lay.

The next Day Mr. Bush happening to be in Company where the Discourse turn- ed on the Excellence of some Capacities,

and

and the readiness of their Wit above
others; " Faith, (faid he) that's true
" enough; for I was in the Fields yefter-
" day, with feveral of my Acquaintance,
" and the Devil a fmart Thing did any
" of them fay but myfelf; and one Thing
" in particular, fo clever, that they all
" fwore they never heaid a better." " In-
" deed!—What was it? (cried one of the
" Company.) — " Why, replied Bufh)
" you muft know that we were all catch-
" ed in a violent Shower, and while we
" ftood under a great Tree, a young
" Lady ran by us; upon which I called
" out to her, Hold! Hold! my dear;
" you had better ftay here, and take fhel-
" ter under a *Hedge:* and as I am a
" living Mah, they all fwore they never
" heard a better Jeft in their Lives."

❖❖❖❖❖❖❖❖❖❖❖❖❖❖❖❖❖❖❖❖❖❖❖

## STORY XII.

### Of a Man who had loft his Ass

A Countryman having loft his Afs,
applied to the Cryer, defiring him
to give Notice of it at the Church-door,
C 2                              which

which he did on three succeſſive Sundays: but no News being heard of the Animal, the Owner deſired the Cryer to continue his Proclamation as uſual, with the Reward of a fat Pig to the finder. The Cryer being an arch Fellow, and tired with the Countryman's Importunity, on a holiday, when the Publick Worſhip was ended, and the People flocked out of the Church, made the following Proclamation. "If there be any Man amongſt "you, who will come forth, and ſolemnly "proteſt he never was in love, he ſhall "have a fat Pig."—On this a fooliſh looibly Fellow, bawled out, "I can ſafe- "ly take my Oath that I am the Perſon "who has never been in love," whereupon the Cryer, taking him by the Sleeve, preſented him to the Countryman, ſaying, "Here, Friend, I have found "your Aſs, the Pig is mine."

STORY

＊❊❊❊❊ ❊❊'❊❊❊❊❊'❊❊❊ ❊❊❊❊❊

## STORY XIII.

### The BLUNDERING PLAYER.

FORTY or Fifty Years ago, when the Actors gave out a New Play, it was cuftomary for them to fay, " Containing the Tragical End of fuch a one, the comical Adventures, the memorable Battle, &c.

Tom Walker, who originally played Mackheath, was giving out a Play, on a Saturday Night, for Mrs. Bicknell's Benefit, when he faid, " Gentlemen and " Ladies, to-morrow Evening will be " perfor—" " To-morrow! (faid a Gen- " tleman in the Pit,) To-morrow will " be Sunday."—Walker was extremely confuled; but recovering himfelt, made a fecond Bow, and proceeded as follows. " Ladies and Gentlemen, On Monday " next, will be performed. the Hiftorical " Play of King Henry the Eighth, con- " taining the Divorce of Anna Bullen,

C 3 " the

" the Marriage of the Princess Catherine,
" and the *Death of Mrs. Bicknell*—for the
Benefit of Cardinal Wolsey.

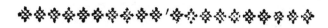

## STORY XIV.

### The Fortunate Family.

IN the Year, 1701, was Born Edward
J⸱⸱⸱ , the Son of a poor Cottager
on the New Forest, Hampshire Ned
being a Boy of bright Parts, was early
taken Notice of by a Gentleman in the
Neighbourhood, who took him into his
Family, as an Assistant to the Gardener.
In this Station he lived about two Years,
when having saved Money enough to
carry him to London, he set out, in the
full Expectation of making his Fortune.
He had not been in Town two Days before
his appearance procured him a Place in
the Family of an eminent Tradesman in
Cornhill. His Business was to pack up,
and carry out small Parcels. This he executed with great Fidelity, and his Master
wished to promote him. but unfortu-
nately

nately, Ned could neither Read nor
Write. These Difficulties were soon got
over by the Education to be obtained at
an Evening School, and Ned was ad-
vanced to the Compting House. In about
Four Years he removed to the Station of
head Clerk to an eminent Merchant, with
whom he continued Five Years, when
the Merchant died, and left him 500l. in
Confideration of his faithful Services,
recommending to him the Care of the
Bufinefs for an only Daughter. This
Truft he faithfully difcharged during
eighteen Months, at the end of which
time the Lady voluntary offered him her
Hand in Marriage. The offer was every
way too agreeable to be rejected. The
Wedding was immediately folemnized,
and our Hero foon became one of the
moft confiderable Merchants in London.
The fruits of this Marriage were two
Sons and two Daughters.—The young
Ladies were both advantageoufly married;
the elder to the Son of a Gentleman juft
returned with a large Fortune from the
Eaft Indies, the younger to the Son of a
wealthy Baronet. The younger Son is
now an eminent Merchant at Briftol, and
the

the elder very deſervedly fills a diſtin-
guiſhed Seat in the Britiſh Houſe of Com-
mons.—Such are the happy Effects of
honeſt Induſtry, and a regular obliging-
neſs of Behaviour.

*XXXXXXXXXXXXXXXXXXXXXXXX*

## STORY XV.

### TRUE and FALSE COURAGE.

DUring the Protectorſhip of Oliver
Cromwell, a young Officer, who
had been bred in France, went to tne
Ordinary at the Black Horſe in Holborn,
where the Perſon that uſually preſided at
table was a rough, old-faſhioned Gentleman, who, according to the cuſtom of
thoſe Times, had been both Major and
Preacher of a Regiment.—The young
Officer was venting ſome new fangled
Notions, and ſpeaking againſt the Diſ-
penſations of Providence. The Major,
at firſt, only deſired him to ſpeak more
reſpectfully of one for whom all the Company had an honour; but finding him
run on in his Extragance, began to repri-
mand him in a more ſerious Manner.
" Young

"Young Man (said he) do not abuse
"your Master while you are eating his
"Bread. Consider whose Air you breathe,
"whose Presence you are in, and who it
"is that gave you the Power of that very
"Speech which you make use of to his
"dishonour." The young Fellow, who
thought to turn Matters to a jest, asked
him if he was going to preach; but at the
same time bid him take care what he said
when he spoke to a Man of Honour. "A
"Man of Honour! (cried the Major)
"thou art an Infidel and a Blasphemer,
"and I shall use thee as such" At length
the Quarrel ran so high that the young
Officer challenged the Major.—On their
coming into the Garden the old Gentleman advised his Antagonist to consider the
Place into which one Pass might drive
him; but finding him grow scurrilous,
"Sirrah (said he) if a thunderbolt does
"not strike thee dead before I come at
"thee, I shall not fail to chastise thee
"for thy Profaneness to thy Maker, and
"thy Sauciness to his Servant."—This
said, he drew his Sword, and cried with
a loud Voice, "The Sword of the Lord
"and of Gideon!" which so terrified our
young

young Gentleman that he was inftantly
difarmed, and thrown on his Knees : In
which Pofture he begged for Life, which
the Major refufed to grant, till he had
afked Pardon for his Offence, in a fhort
extempore Prayer, which the Major dic-
tated on the Spot, and the other repeated,
in the prefence of the whole Company,
which was by this time affembled in the
Garden.

## STORY XVI.

### Of the KING of NAPLES, and the CHE-
### VALIER de ST. GEORGE.

ON the 24th of Auguft 1734. a fleet
of Ships failed from Naples for Sici-
ly, with a fair Wind.—While the Che-
valier was attending the Embarkation, a
blaft of Wind blew his Hat into the Sea.
Several Officers immediately endeavoured
to take it up ; but he called out, " Let it
" alone ; I will go and get another in
" England ;" whereupon the King of
Naples, throwing his Hat into the Sea,
faid, " And I will go with you" on which
a ftander-

a ftander-by remarked, that " they might
" go bare-headed a long time, if they
" got no Hats till they went to England
" for them; and befides, they would
" find none there that would fit their
" Heads."

✿✿✿✿✿✿✿✿✿✿✿✿✿✿✿✿✿✿✿✿✿✿✿✿✿

## STORY XVII.

### The JOURNEYMAN BAKER.

A Journeyman, who lived with a capi-
tal Baker in the City of London,
fucceeded to an Eftate of 1500 l. a Year.
Having taken Poffeffion, he invited his
Mafter and Miftrefs to his Country Seat;
and, at parting, told them, that, as he
had the Eftate of a Gentleman, he would
aim at the Qualifications; for which Pur-
pofe he would make the Tour of Europe.
The Idea he had conceived of the Advan-
tages arifing from Travel, made him deaf
to the Remonftrances of his Friends, who
forefaw the ruin of his Eftate: But he
anfwered them, " that he had a good
" Trade in his Belly, and could never
                                    " break,

" bieak, till he broke his neck."—His
Expences Abroad made a confiderable
rent in his Estate, which after his return,
he foon ran through entirely.—When all
was fpent, he engaged again with his for-
mer Master, and when his old Acquaintance ask'd him what he could think
when he acted fo imprudently, he would
fay "Why? I thought of nothing but
" my Pleafure, and have gratified my
" Inclinations while it lasted, and now
" it is gone, has left me this Advantage,
" that I have feen more of the World
" than any Journeyman Baker in Town,
" and I din'd at my Master's Table,
" which I never did before "

STORY XVIII.

The Widow's Exchange.

A Young Lady having buried an old
Husband, whom she married for
Money, employed a Carver to make a
Statue of Wood, as much like him as
possible, which, with feeming regard to
his

his Memory, she placed every Night by her Side in Bed. A young Gentleman, who was enamoured of the Widow, one Night, bribed the Maid to permit him to lay in old Simon's Place. The Widow went to Bed, and, as usual, threw her Arms across the Figure, (as she thought it) of her dear Husband, and, finding it warm, crept still closer, till she was convinced it was a better Bedfellow than Old Simon. In the Morning the Maid called, as usual, to know what she would have for Dinner. "Why, (said "she) dress the Turkey that was brought "in Yesterday, roast a Leg of Mutton, "with Cauliflower, and get a handsome "Dish of Fish."—"Madam, (said the "Maid) we have not Wood enough to "dress so much Victuals.—"Why then "(cried the Mistress) you must e'en "burn Old Simon."

D            STORY

## STORY XIX.

### Old Dobson's Cross.

AN old Country Fellow, who was married to a perfect Termagant, going one Sunday to Church, heard the Minister preach from the following Words.—" Take up your Cross and fol-" low me" Dobson was extremely atten-tive to the Discourse, and as soon as Church was done, went home, and taking his Wife on his Back by force, ran as fast as he was able after the Parson, who seeing how the Fellow was loaded, asked him the Reason " Why, what a plague, " cries Dobson, has your Reverence for-" got already?—Did not your Worship " bid us take up our Cross, and follow " you? and I am sure this is the greatest " Cross that I have in the World, an' " please ye."

STORY

✱✱✱✱✱✱✱✱✱✱✱✱✱✱✱✱✱✱✱✱✱

## STORY XX.

### Anecdote of an Earl of St. Alban's.

THE Earl of St. Alban's, Secretary to Queen Henrietta Maria, in all her Misfortunes, found himself at the Restoration but in an indifferent Condition. Being one Day with Charles the Second, when all Distinctions were laid aside, a Stranger came with an importunate Suit for an Employment of great Value, which was just vacant. The King ordered him to be admitted, and bid the Earl personate himself. The Gentleman addressed himself accordingly; innumerated his Services to the Royal Family, and hoped the grant of the Place would not be deemed too great a Reward. " By no Means (replied the Earl) and I " am only sorry that, as soon as I heard " of the Vacancy, I conferred it on my " faithful Friend there, the Earl of St. " Alban's—(pointing at the King) who " has constantly followed the Fortunes

.      D 2       " both

" both of my Father and myself, and has
" hitherto gone ungratified : — but when
" any thing of this kind happens again,
" worthy your acceptance, pray let me
" see you."— The Gentleman withdrew,
—the King smiled at the jest, and con-
firmed the Grant to the Earl.

�֍✦✧✦✧✦✧✦✧✦✧✦✧✦✧✦✧✦✧✦✧

# STORY XXI.

### HARDINESS of a FRENCH OFFICER.

THIS Gentleman being sent from
the Camp to the Court, during a
hard Frost, had no sooner delivered his
Letters to the King, than the Chamber-
lain of the Houshold appointed him a
Lodging in the Palace, as he was to return to the Camp the next Day. But he
refused it, saying, " It becomes not me
" to lie on a Bed of down, when my Ge-
" neral, and the whole Army are forced
" to sleep on the frozen Earth."—So saying, he ordered some Straw out of the
Stables, and slept in the open Air.—The
King, hearing of the Circumstance, made
him

him a handsome Present, and recommended him to the General, as one of the bravest Men in his Army.

## S T O R Y XXII.

### The Fortunate Soldier.

IN the Reign of Queen Anne a young Fellow in the County of Berks, being disgusted with a Woman that his Father had chosen for him as a Wife, enlisted in a Marching Regiment then recruiting at Reading. As his Education and Manner of Behaviour was superior to that of his fellow Soldiers, he was soon distinguished by his Officers, and, before he had been a Month in the Service, he was promoted to the Rank of Corporal, and ere three Months had elapsed was made a Serjeant. In this Station he continued for two Years —was then raised to be Serjeant-Major, and from that Station to an Ensigncy.— The Regiment was now order'd into Flanders, and in the famous Battle of Ramillies, our young Ensign had the honour

D 3                          of

of faving his Colours from the refolute attack of four French Soldiers. In reward of this gallant defence he was promoted to the Rank of a Lieutenant, and from thence he fucceeded to that of a Captain, in this ftation he continued many years, with equal Honour to himfelf, and his Country, 'till having received a challenge from a Brother Officer, (on a fuppofed trifling offence) he had the virtue to refufe it; which coming to the knowledge of his then Sovereign George II. his Majefty promoted him to the Rank of a Colonel; faying that a Man of approved valour would be inexcufable in rifking his Life to comply with an arbitrary and inhuman Cuftom.

## STORY XXIII.

### A SPANISH LADY'S REVENGE.

A Few Years fince an Englifh Gentleman, who, in a rencounter by Night in the Streets of Madrid, had the Misfortune to kill his Man, fled into a
Church

Church Porch for Sanctuary. Leaning against the Door, he was surprized to find it open, and a glimmering light in the Church. He had the Courage to advance towards the Light; but was terribly startled at the Sight of a Woman in White, who ascended from a Grave with a bloody Knife in her Hand. The Phantom walked up to him, and asked him what he did there. He believed he had met a Ghost, and told her the Truth, without reserve; on which she addressed him as follows;
" Stranger thou art in my Power: I am
" a Murderer as thou art. I am a Nun
" of a noble Family. A base perjured
" Man undid me, and boasted of it. I
" soon had him dispatched, but not content
" with the Murder, I have bribed
" the Sexton to let me enter his Grave,
" and have now plucked out his false
" Heart from his Body, and thus I use
" the Traitor's Heart."—Thus saying,
" she tore it in Pieces, and trampled it
" under her Feet."—This Story, however
Romantick it may appear, hath been
vouched for Truth.

STORY

***************/****************

## STORY XXIV.

The Jew's Stratagem to save his Life.

SAladin, the Soldan of Babylon, living
at too profuse a rate, and being at
the same time engaged in a War with
several European Powers, found his trea-
sures very much exhausted. Extraordinary
matters happening, he had pressing occa-
sions for Money, and not know'ng how to
raise it thought of applying to a rich Jew,
who lent Money at Interest. He was,
however, afraid that the Jew would refuse
him, and at the same time unwilling to
oblige him to do it, or to Punish him in
case of refusal, without a colourable
pretence for so doing. He therefore sent
for him, received him with complaisance,
and addressed him as follows. " I am
" told that you are a wise Man, and very
" knowing in matters of Religion. Pray
" which of these three do you think the
" best, the Jewish, the Saracen, or the
" Christian ?"—The Jew saw the Snare
that

that was laid for him, and rightly judged
that he fhould be entrapped, if he preſer-
red either Religion to the other. He
therefore made the following anſwer.
" The queſtion that you aſk me, my Lord,
" is very curious; but before you com-
" mand me to declare my opinion, permit
" to tell you a Story. I remmember I
" have heard of a rich Man, who beſides
" other precious things had a Ring of great
" value; and being proud of Poſſeſſing ſo
" rare a Jewel, leſt it to his Poſter ty as a
" monument of his great Riches, and
" ordered by his Will, that whichſoever
" of his Sons ſhould, after his death, be
" found poſſeſs'd of this Ring, ſhould in-
" herit all his Eſtate, and be reſpected as
" the head of his Family. In proceſs of
" time the Ring paſſed through many
" Hands, till at laſt it came to one who
" had three Sons equally dutiful, wiſe,
" and obedient to their Father, who
" loving them all alike, had, at different
" times, given them all reaſon to expect
" it; and at length contrived to ſatisfy
" all three. To effect this, he procured
" an ingenious artiſt to make two other
" Rings, ſo like the true one, that no
                                    " difference

"difference could be seen. The Father
"died—Every one had his Ring; and
"each tried, by Law, to get Possession
"of the Estate which he imagined to be
"his due; and it yet remains undecided
"who shall inherit it. It is, my Lord,
"the same thing with regard to the three
"Religions given by God, to the People
"you have mentioned. Every one believes
"that he is the Heir of God, has his true
"Laws, and obeys his Commandments:
"But which was in possession was never
"yet determined."—Saladin, seeing that
the Jew had avoided the Net which was
spread for him, told him of his Necessities,
begged his assistance and added, that he
intended to have compelled the Payment,
if his discreet answer had not prevented
him. The Jew readily lent him the
Money which Saladin faithfully repaid;
conceived a great affection for him, and
maintained him honourably at Court for
the rest of his Life.

STORY

ANECDOTES, CHARACTERS, WHIMS, and
ODDITIES.

HARRY NICKIT, is a Yeoman,
of about 100 l. a Year, an honeſt
Man. He is juſt within the Game Act,
and qualified to kill a Hare or a Pheaſant.
He knocks down a Dinner with his Gun
twice or thrice a Week; and by that
Means lives much cheaper than thoſe who
have not ſo good an Eſtate as himſelf. He
would be a good Neighbour if he did not
deſtroy ſo many Partridges: In ſhort, he
is a very ſenſible Man, ſhoots flying, and
has been ſeveral times Foreman of the
Petty Jury.

TOM TOUCHY is a Fellow famous for
*taking the Law* of every body. There is
not one in the Town where he lives that
he has not ſued at Quarter-Seſſions His
Head is full of Coſts, Damages, and
Ejectments. He plagued a couple of honeſt Gentlemen ſo long for a Treſpaſs in
breaking one of his Hedges, till he was
forced

forced to fell the Ground it inclofed, to
defray the Charges of the Profecution.
His Father left him Fourfcore Pounds a
Year; but he has caft and been caft fo
often, that he is not worth Thirty.

KATE WILLOW is a witty, mifchievous
Wench, who was a Beauty   She was fo
flippant with her Anfwers to all the honeft
Fellows that came near her, and fo very
Vain of her Beauty, that fhe has valued
herfelf upon her Charms till they are
ceafed.  She therefore now makes it her
bufinefs to prevent other young Women
from being more difcreet than fhe was
herfelf.

HARRY TESETT and his Lady, are a
very extraordinary Couple.  Harry in the
Days of his Celibacy, was one of thofe
pert Creatures, who have much Vivacity,
and little Underftanding.  Mrs. Rebecca
Quickley, whom he married, had all the
Fire of Youth and a lively manner could
do towards making an agreeable Woman.
Thefe two People of feeming merit fell
into each others Arms, and Paffion being
fated, and no good fenfe in either to fuc-
ceed

ceed it, their Life is now at a ſtand, their Meals are inſipid and their Time tedious; their Fortune has placed them above Care, and their loſs of Taſte reduced them below Diverſion.

The Son of RURICOLA (whoſe Life was one continued ſeries of worthy Actions, and Gentleman-like Inclinations,) is the Companion of drunken Clowns, and knows no Senſe of Praiſe but what he receives from his own Servants. His pleaſures are mean and inordinate, his Language baſe and filthy, His Behaviour rough and abſurd.

✕✕✕✕✕✕✕✕✕✕✕✕✕✕✕✕✕✕ ✕✕✕✕✕✕✕✕

The following Order of QUEEN ELIZA-ᴮᴇᴛʜ, for the Gift of her old Cloaths to her Maids of Honour, and others, will-be deemed a great Curioſity.

ELIZABETH by the Grace of God, Quene of Englande, France, and Irelande, defender of the Faith &c. To all and ſingular to whom theiſe ſhall come, greating, knowe ye, that our truſtie

E                                           and

and well beloved fervants, John Roynor
and Ralph Hoope, yeomen of our
guarderobe of roobes, hath delyverid by
our commandemt oute of their custodye
and charge, att divers and fundry tymes,
all fuche pcell of stuff by us gevon to
fundry pfons whose names enfue as more
plavnelye hereafter doth appere, that is
to faye first ——gevon to the lady Katheryn Grey, oone open gowne of black vellat, layed on with three pafsamayne lafes,
faced with unfhorne vellat, and edged
with a frenge; lyned througheowte with
black farceonet.

*Item,* Gevon to the lady Cobham,
oone loose gowne of black fattin rased
allong, with a garde of black vellat,
ftyched byas cutt, and ravelid; and
edgid, with a frenge, lyned with farcco-
net and fuftian,—and oone round kyrtle
of black wrought vellat, edged with a
frenge, and lyned with ferceonett,—and
a'fo one perycoate of crimfon vellat with
a ftyched garde, lyned with cotton and
fuftian.

*Iter,*

*Item*, Gevon to the lady Carew, one Frenche kyrtle of purple wrought vellat, with a fatten grounde, and lyned with Taphata.

*Item*, Taken by the faid John Roynor and Ralf Hoope, oone night gowne paft our wearing, of black vellat, weltid with a midhank welte of vellat, ftyched with filk, furred with callabar, and edged with luzerne.

*Item*, Gevon to Kathetyn Cary, oone gowne of ruffet fatten, weltid downeright with black vellat; with ruffe of ruffet ta phata round, all about.

*Item*, Gevon to Dorothy Brodebelte, oone open gowne of Ruffet wrought Vellat the Grounde Satten, with brode weltes whiped over with a Satten wrothe, edgid with a frenge, and lyned with farceonett, and faced with pynked taffata, and oone petycoate of vellat ftryped with golde, the fkyrts lined with purple farceonett.

*Item*, Gevon to Elizabeth Sands, oone open gowne of prented fatten, garded with vellat, and lyned with taffata.

*Item*, **Gevon** to Elizabeth Sloo, oone gowne of black pinked vellat, borderid abóute with three fwelling welts cutt and raved, lyned with taphata, and edgid with a frenge.

*Item*, **Gevon** to a Tartarian Woman, oone loofe Gown of blak taphata, weltid-byas with blak vellat, on either fide of the welt a purled lafe of filk, lined with taphata, one French kyrtle of ruffet fatten, lyned with ruffett taphata; oone loofe gowne of black taphata, with a brode garde of vellat, layed on with whiped lafe and Bruffels work lafe, lyned with blak taphata; and one Frenche kyrtle 'of blak fattin, weltid with vellat, and lyned with taphata.

*Item*, **Delyverd** to Katheryn Afhteley, by her to be employed in panying of Cu-fhions, one Frenche Gowne of purple vel-lat, lyned with purple taffata, with a peire of wide fleves to the fame.

*Item*, **Taken** by the faid John Rovnor and Rauf Hoope, oone night gowne paft our wearing, of black fatten, with two Yards of vellat, with a fienge lafe layed
upon

upon the edge of the ga,d, furred with
lybards, and lafed with luzerne.

All which ftuff, and every part and
pcell thereof we do knowlede to have
been delyvird fince the laft of January,
an° fecond° mihi, in manner and tourme
abovefaid, by the faid John Roynoi and
Raef Hoope, and thereof do acquet, and
difcharge the faid John and Raef, their
heres, executors, and adminiftiators, by
theife pfents, againft us, our heires and fuc-
ceffors.

Goven under our Signett att our mannor
at Grenewithe, the 16 May the thirde
yere of our reigne, 1560.

⁎⁎ The Original, in the Queen's own
hand writing, was, about twenty Years
ago, in the poffeffion of Mr. Jo'eph In-
gram, Linnen Draper, in Cheapfide.—
It is remaikable that her Majefty fpells the
name Ralph four different ways in the
above Inftrument.

SINGULAR CUSTOM.
A practice of a very extraordinary na-
ture with regard to marriage prevailed
E 3                    among

among the Lacedemonians, who looked upon that Inftitution as of fo high importance to Society, that they allowed their Women to beat all the old Batchelors Publickly once a Year.

## Venetian Gallantry.

The gallantry that preceeds marriage, among the Venetians, has fomething very remarkable in it.—When all things are adjufted between the parties, the Gallant muft Walk every Evening, at ftated Hours, before his Miftrefs's Windows.— When the Bridegroom makes a vifit to his Bride, he is obliged to carry her the Pearl Necklace, which he is to make her a prefent of.

## Spanish Custom.

In Spain a Man has often a Wife, a Miftrefs and a Concubine, all which is tolerated and does not occafion any manner of difturbance in Families.

Jack Truepenny has unrefifted good-nature, which makes him incapable of having

having a Property in any thing. His Fortune, his reputation, his Time, and his Capacity are at any Man's Service that comes first. When he was at School he was whipped thrice a Week for faults he took upon himself to excuse others; and once, when a Friend of his had suffered in a Vice of the Town, all the Physick his Friend took was conveyed to him by Jack, and inscribed, "A Bolus or an Electuary for Mr. Truepenny." Jack had a good Estate left to him which came to nothing; because he believed all who pretended to demands upon it. This easiness and credulity destroy all the other merit he has; and he has all his Life been a Sacrifice to others without ever receiving thanks, or doing one good action.

MR. WORTHY is an old Man who passes for an Humourist, and one who does not understand the Figure he ought to make in the World, while he lives in a Lodging of ten Shillings a Week, with only one Servant: while he dresses himself in Cloth or Stuff, according to the Season, and has no one necessary Attention to any thing but the Bell which calls to Prayers

twice

twice a day. This Gentleman gives away
all which is the overplus of a great Fortune,
by secret methods, to other Men. If he
has not the pomp of a numerous train,
and of professors of Service to him, he
has, every Day he lives, the consciousness
that the Widow, the Fatherless, the
Mourner, and the Stranger; bless his un-
seen Hand in their Prayers. He gives up
all the Compliments which People of his
own Condition could make him, for the
Pleasures of helping the afflicted, sup-
plying the needy, and befriending the
neglected. He keeps to himself much
more than he wants, and gives a vast refuse of his Superfluities to purchase Heaven, and by freeing others from the temp-
tations of Worldly want, to carry a retinue
with them thither.

WILL. FUNNELL, the Toper who is
now in the decline of Life, frequently
amuses himself with reckoning up how
much Liquor has past through him
in the last twenty Years, which, according
to his computation, amounts to twenty
three Hogsheads of October, four Tuns
of Port, half a Kilderkin of small Beer,

Nineteen

Nineteen Barrels of Cyder, and three
glaffes of Champaigne ; befides which he
has affifted at Seven Hundred Bowls of
Punch, not to mention Drams and
whets without Number. What a glori-
ous Ambition is that of *Funnell* to become
at once equally abfurd and wicked :—to
give himfelf daily pain, merely to promote
a certain Suicide.

FLAVIA is ever well dreffed, and always
the genteeleft Woman you meet : but the
make of her mind very much contributes
to the ornament of her body  She has
the greateft fimplicity of Manners of any
of her fex.  This makes every thing look
native about her, and her Cloaths are fo
exactly fitted, that they appear as it were
part of her Perfon.  Every one that fees
her knows her to be of Quality ; but her
diftinction is owing to her Manne, and
not to her habit.  Her Beauty is full of
Attraction, but not of Allurement. There
is fuch a compofure in her Looks, and pro-
priety in her Drefs, that you would think
it impoffible fhe fhould change the garb
you one Day fee her in, for any thing fo
becoming, till you next Day fee her in,
another.

another. There is no other Myftery in this, but that however fhe is Apparaled, fhe is herfelt the fame. for there is fo immediate a Relation between our Thoughts and Gueftures, that a Woman muft *think* well to *look* well.

ORSON THICKSET is a meer Huntf-man, whofe Father's Death, and fome Difficulties about Legacies, brought out of the Woods to Town, He was at that time one of thofe Country Savages who defpife the Softnefs they meet in Town and Court, and profefledly fhew their Strength and roughnefs in every Motion and Gefture, in Scorn of bowing and cringing. He was, at his firft Appearance, remarkable for that Piece of good Breeding peculiar to Englifhmen, *Defiance,* and fhewed every one he met he was as good a Man as he.

Mrs. GATTY is an agreeable, Mrs. *Frontlet* an awful Beauty. Thefe Ladies are perfect Friends, from a Knowledge that their Perfections are too different to ftand in Competition. He that likes Gatty

can

can have no relish for so solemn a Crea-
ture, as Frontlet; and an Admirer of
Frontlet will call Gatty a May-pole Girl.
Gatty for ever smiles upon you, and
Frontlet disdains to see you smile. Gatty's
Love is a shining quick Flame; Frontlet's a slow wasting Fire. Gatty likes the
Man that diverts her; Frontlet him who
adores her. Gatty always improves the
Soil in which she travels; Frontlet lays
waste the Country. Gatty does not only
smile, but laughs at her Lover; Frontlet
not only looks Serious, but Frowns at him.
Still the Men of wit and Coxcombs their
followers are professed Servants of Gatty:
the Politicians, and pretenders to Politicks,
give solemn worship to Frontlet. Their
reign will be best judged by its Duration:
Frontlet will never be chosen more; and
Gatty is a Toast for Life,

PAULO and AVARO are two wealthy
Merchants; but they differ in the use and
application of their Riches, which you
immediately see upon entering their Doors.
The Habitation of Paulo has at once the
air of a Nobleman and a Merchant. You
see the Servants act with affection to their
Master

Master and satisfaction to themselves: The
Master meets you with an open Counte-
nance, full of Benevolence and Integrity.
Your Business is dispatched with all that
confidence and welcome, which always
accompanies honest Minds: his Table is
the Image of Plenty and Generosity, sup-
ported by Justice and Frugality —But if
you enter the House of Avaro, out comes
an awkward Fellow with a careful Coun-
tenance,—Sir, would you speak with my
Master.—May I crave your name?—
After the first preamble, he leads you into
a Noble Solitude, a great House that seems
uninhabited, but from the end of the
spacious Hall moves toward you Avaro,
with a suspicious aspect, as if he believed
you a Thief; nor would you, when you
approach him, take him for any thing better than a Pick Pocket.—Paulo grows
wealthy by being a common good ;
Avaro by being a general Evil. Paulo has
the Art, Avaro the craft of trade.—When
Paulo gains, all Men he deals with are
the better. Whenever Avaro profits, another certainly loses  In a word, *Paulo*
is a CITIZEN, and *Avaro* a CIT.

Epitaph

### Epitaph on Sir JOHN HILL.

#### I.

ENtomb'd beneath this humble stone,
 A learned Knight is laid,
Who fav'd our Lives, and loft his own,
 In the due courfe of trade.

#### II.

*Bardana* for the Gout he fold,
 Nor fear'd th' effects of age,
For who, faid he, can e'er grow old
 That *Tincture* drinks of *Sage?*

#### III.

For every Ill of every kind,
 A Remedy he fought,
And cur'd all People but the blind, —
 For thofe were blind who bought.

#### IV.

Dear *Doctor*—*Botanift*—farewell,
 *Scribler* and *Player* Adieu !
Or rife to Heaven, or fink to Hell,
 You'll find no more like you.

### EXTEMPORE ; on a *Lame Poet.*

CEafe, Scribler, longer to torment us,
 Thou ne'er can'ft gain the path to Fame ;
One of the Curfes Heaven has fent us,
Is Verfe that's like the Writer—lame.

F
        On

### On an Old Lady appearing at Drury Lane Theatre, with a high Head Dress of Feathers.

GRizetta, Copying youthful Sinners,
    Proves her ideas to be frail,
And tells us, while she wags her pinners,
    She wishes but to wag her tail.

#### II.

Each Childish folly is forgiven,
    When Youth and Beauty pow'rful plead;
But Lovers seek another Heaven
    Than Feathers on an Ancient Head.

### CHRISTMAS DAY, a Song.

#### I.

LADS and Lasses raise your Voices,
    Strike, O Muse, the sprightliest lay;
All within the Muse's choice is,
    While she Sings of Christmas Day.

#### II.

Pies and Puddings now are plenty,
    Ham and Veal, and Beef and Chicken;
Chines and Turkies too are sent ye,
    Would you wish for better Picking.

#### III.

Play the Cards, and fill the Glasses,
    Drink about, and Sing, and Play;
All the Lads, and all the Lasses,
    Revel thus on Christmas Day.

### LEAP YEAR, A New Song.

#### I.

MAIDS attend to my Song,
It shall not hold you long;
I Sing for the Year Seventy Six;
While unmarried you be,
Take example from me,
And look cautiously round er'e you fix.

#### II.

Let the Man whom you chuse,
Have Wit to amuse,
And prudence and Sense to advise;
For his Person—no matter,
But if he should flatter
O guide not your hearts by your Eyes.

#### III.

In Leap—Year, they say,
Young Maids go astray,
And are apt to be courting the Men;
Then guard you this Year,
And the next, never fear,
Your Swains will address you again.

### The ROSE, A New Song.

#### I.

AS blooms the Rose in May's gay Month,
And flourishes in June,
So bloom the Fair of Britain's Isle,
And reach bright Beauty's noon.

## II.

As shrinks the Flower beneath the cold,
　And shuns the blighting Wind,
So Reputation's left, unless,
　There's Virtue in the Mind.

## III

Beauty's a short and transient bloom,
　And like the Rose decays,
But Virtue still encreasing lives,
　And brightens all our Days.

Chloe's Likeness—an Epigrammatic Song.

## I.

WHat's Chloe like? young Damon Cries,
　　I ne'er saw such a creature,
The Stars of Heav'n are like her Eyes,
　A Sun—beam is each Feature.

## I

Colin, who Damon's whim did strike,
　Replies, in merry part,
" There's nothing, Friend, your Chloe's like,
　" Except—to break your heart"

The PLAYHOUSE, a New Song

## I

THE Theatre is but a Picture of Life,
　　Where every one crouds for a seat,
Tho' few, after all their contention and strife,
　Are contented with those that they get.

II.

## II.

The Gods, whom a Shilling sticks under the Roof,
  Would fain with their betters sit down,
Yet thinking their Shilling is Money enough,
  Laugh at him who deposits his Crown.

## III.

The Cit in the Gallery, the Rake in the Pit,
  Despising each others false taste;
The Rake thinks the Cit is a Miser—the Cit,
  Knows the Cash of the Rake runs to waste.

## IV.

The gay painted Dame in the Slips we behold,
  Who plays her full game at the Ball,
While the Manager pockets his Customer's Gold,
  And fairly laughs at them all

Song in the New Entertainment of the SULTAN.

## I.

BLEST Hero, whom in peace and War,
  Triumph alike, and raise our wonder;
In peace the shafts of Love you bear,
  In War the bolts of Jove's own Thunder.

## II.

Venus and Mars yet never strove,
  To make a Name so great in story,
Still Victor in the lists of Love,
  As Conqueror in the fields of Glory.

New

### NEW JESTS, BLUNDERS, &c.

A Middlesex Farmer had lost Three Heifers, on which he set the Crier to work, who proclaimed that Farmer —— had lost Three Heifers, Two of which were Cows. A Gentleman who stood by, cried, "That's a Bull!"—"True (said the Cryer) I'm much obliged t'ye Sir,—One of 'em was a Bull."

A young Lady, whose Name was *Pye*, was asked what she was like: She answered, "like a Common Dish at Christmas."—"No (said a Gentleman.")—"Not till you are *Minced*.

"What's my Thoughts like? (said a Macaroni) —"Like yourself," replied a Lady, "next to nothing."

"The Turks (said a Lady) are allowed as many "Wives as they can maintain.—On the contrary, "an Englishman is unwilling to marry, till he "knows whether his Bride has Fortune sufficient "to maintain herself."

Mr. Foote was in Company when it was observed that the Ladies liked Mr. Foote. "True (said another) but Mr. Foote does not like the "Ladies."

A Lady sitting with her Husband, on a Thursday Night, said "My dear, your Horns are budding

ding."—Then (faid he) I'll go to Smithfield to-
" morrow, with the reft of the Calves."

A Gentleman meeting 26 Geefe on Finchley
Common, exclaimed " Here comes my Lord
" Mayor, and the Court of Aldermen."

A Man telling a moft improbable Story, another
faid—" As you relate it, Sir, I believe it ; but if
" I had told it myfelf I'll be d—d if I fhould have
" given credit to it."

An Irifhman having purchafed a Ticket, told
the Lottery Office Keeper that if he would enfure
it a Prize, he'd give him the value of a Blank for
his Trouble.

A young Lady was faying fhe would give any
thing fhe had for a good Hufband. "Then (faid
" a Gentleman) you'll not be long fingle. You
" have fomething to give, that no Hufband will
" refufe."

The famous Joe Miller was told that his whole
Life was a *Jeft*. " That may be, (faid he) but I
" find it a very *ferious Bufinefs* to Live."

A Man being afked his Profeffion, faid, " I'm
" a Shoemaker by Religion, and a Drunkard by
" Trade."

The late Lord Chefterfield being afked his Opinion of a very gay and talkative Woman, faid fhe
was like a Parrot—All Feathers and Noife.

when

When the difpute arofe about the bad Halfpence, a ... ... Lord, who was addreffed by a Gentleman, faid ... had no Objection to him, but that he was a ... ...

The ... Mr. Whitfield was once invited to Dinner among fome Noblemen, and defired to fay Grace. "It will be in vain, (faid he) you are "all GRACELESS."

> T ... ve we given our little ftore,
> Nor with our Readers afk for more,
> A fh ... ing buys the curious Book
> We've took fuch wondrous Pains to Cook.
> N ... Your dear Readers, if you're willing,
> We ... you for another Shilling.

On the 1ft of *February*, 1775. will be publifhed,

# A NEW MAGAZINE,

On a Plan which it is humbly hoped will obtain, the Approb ... ion of the Public.

*⁎* Such Ladies and Gentlemen as may chufe to fa ... ... with their Correfpondence, will pleafe, to direct to the Editors, at G. ... LLI's, No. 59. Paternofter Row. London.

CPSIA information can be obtained
at www.ICGtesting.com
Printed in the USA
BVHW030153140922
646992BV00003B/25